AF575420

Don't Look a Gift Horse in the Mouth!

by Cynthia Amoroso ★ illustrated by Mernie Gallagher-Cole

Wonder Books
An Imprint of The Child's World®
childsworld.com

Published by The Child's World®
800-599-READ • childsworld.com

ISBN Information
9781503865600 (Reinforced Library Binding)
9781503866058 (Portable Document Format)
9781503866898 (Online Multi-user eBook)
9781503867734 (Electronic Publication)

LCCN 2022939492

Printed in the United States of America

ABOUT THE AUTHOR

As a daughter of elementary and English teachers, Cynthia Amoroso grew up in a home that was filled with language. She spent many hours enjoying reading and writing. Later, she followed in the footsteps of both her parents and became a teacher. As a high school English teacher and as an elementary teacher, Cynthia shared her love of language with students. She has always been fascinated with idioms and other figures of speech as they reflect and represent the culture and people who use them.

ABOUT THE ILLUSTRATOR

Mernie Gallagher-Cole lives in Pennsylvania with her husband and children. She uses idioms like the ones in this book every day. She has illustrated many children's books as well as greeting cards, puzzles, and games.

Contents

People use **idioms** every day. These are sayings and phrases with meanings that are different from the actual words. Some idioms seem silly. Many of them don't make much sense . . . at first.

This book will help you understand some of the most common idioms. The illustrations will show you how you might hear a saying or phrase. And the accompanying examples and definitions will tell you how the idiom is used, what it really means, and where it **originated**. All of these idioms—even the silly or humorous ones—are a rich, colorful part of the English language. You'll soon see that understanding idioms and knowing how to use them is a piece of cake!

Achilles' heel

The baseball game between the Eagles and the Panthers was in the ninth inning. The Eagles were one run ahead, but the Panthers' best hitter was up to bat. Mike, the Eagles' pitcher, was nervous. His coach walked out to the mound.

"I saw this kid play last week," the coach said. "Throw him a curveball—that's his Achilles' heel."

MEANING: *A person's area of weakness; the one fault or flaw or* ***vulnerable*** *spot*

ORIGIN: *Achilles is a famous hero and warrior from Greek mythology. According to the myth, Achilles' mother dipped her infant son into the River Styx to magically protect him from harm. However, she held him by his heel, which left that part of his body unprotected. Years later Achilles was killed by an enemy who shot a poison arrow into his heel.*

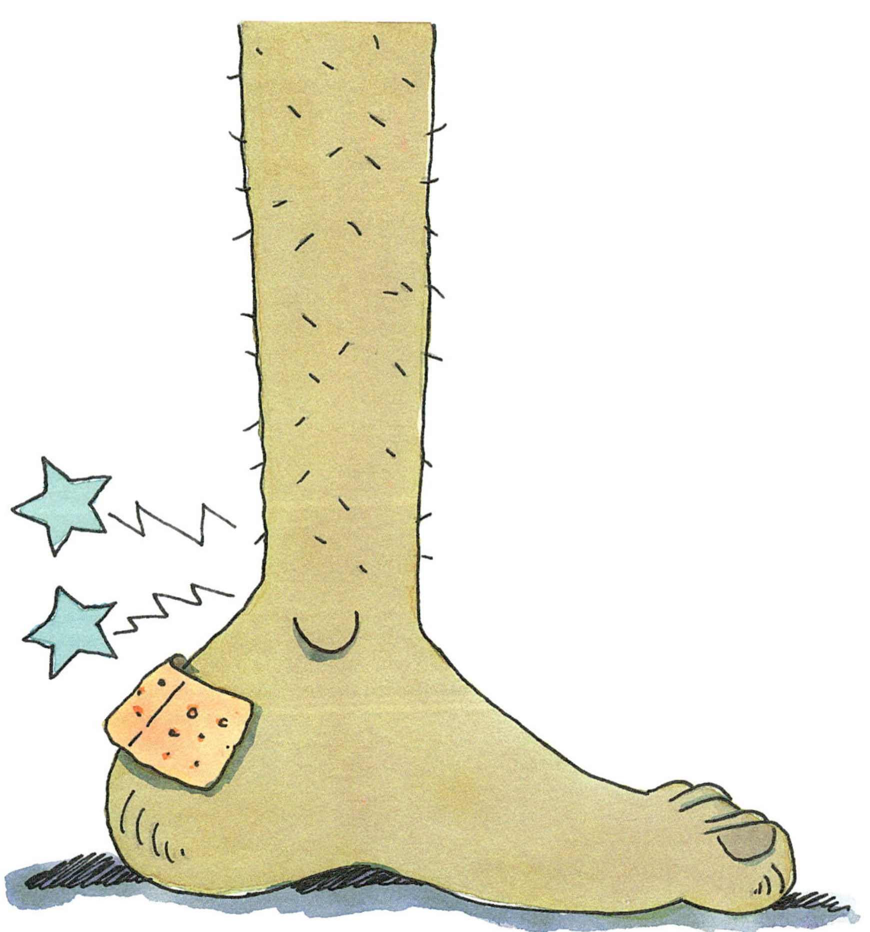

Busy as a bee

Hannah's grandmother was a great gardener, and Hannah loved helping her. Hannah learned how to hoe and weed, and she had fun picking strawberries and green beans.

"Grandma, I'm going inside to get a drink. Do you want something?" asked Hannah.

"I'd love some lemonade," replied Grandma. "We'll sit together and rest. You've been as busy as a bee!"

MEANING: *To be very busy getting things done; very active*

ORIGIN: *This popular saying dates back to the 1500s. Bees are known to be busy, constant workers. Comparing people to "busy bees" was a common description in literature and poetry.*

The chips are down

Jamie and his dad were watching their hometown football team try to win a close game. The coach had called a time out and was talking to the players.

"There's only time for one more play," said Jamie. "Do you think they can score?"

"Keep an eye on Burnside, the wide receiver," said Dad. "When the chips are down, he's the best choice. Nobody does better under pressure."

MEANING: *An urgent situation; when someone has one last chance to make something work*

ORIGIN: *The saying originated in the United States during the early 1800s. The "chips" refer to gambling, most likely the game of poker. In poker, a person places bets with chips, which represent money. When a player's pile of chips is down, it means the player is low on money and losing.*

Don't look a gift horse in the mouth

Katie's cousin had just bought a new computer and given Katie her old one.

"It works OK," said Katie, "but it's not as nice as the one I wanted."

"It's not quite as fast," Dad agreed, "but it's still pretty nice, and it didn't cost us a cent. Don't look a gift horse in the mouth!"

MEANING: *To accept and appreciate a gift, even if you're not sure about it*

ORIGIN: *A version of this* ***proverb*** *dates back to the 1500s. You can get a good idea of a horse's age by looking at its teeth. In those days a person buying a horse would examine its teeth to make sure they were getting a healthy, young horse. The phrase soon applied to gift-giving. If you are examining a gift too closely, it is likely to be considered rude or insulting to the person who gave it to you.*

Dropping like flies

The dance finals were tomorrow, but things weren't looking good for Grace's team. The flu was going around, and Grace had been sick for two days. The phone rang, and a few minutes later, Grace's sister walked into the room.

"Bad news," she said. "Ms. Wilkins says your teammates are dropping like flies! Three more dancers have gotten sick."

MEANING: *When a number of people leave or drop out from an activity*

ORIGIN: *The first known use of this* ***expression*** *was in a publication in 1902. The exact origin is unknown, but most people believe it refers to the very short life span of a fly.*

Elbow grease

Nikki's parents were looking for a new house. One day, they came home really excited.

"We found it!" Mom said. "It's a great place. Come on, we'll take a ride and show you."

"Ew, what's that smell?" Nikki asked when she walked inside. "This house is pretty dirty!"

"Yeah, it's a bit musty," Dad agreed. "All it needs is a little elbow grease. Come look at this great backyard!"

MEANING: *Hard physical work*

ORIGIN: *This idiom dates back to Great Britain during the late 1600s. The "elbow grease" refers to a person's sweat as they were scrubbing a floor or polishing a surface for a long time.*

A fish out of water

"What a day!" Mom sighed as she put down her bag.

"What happened?" asked Nate.

"I helped teach some programs for first-graders," answered Mom. "I'm exhausted!"

"Why? You're used to teaching," Nate said.

"Well, I'm used to teaching high school students!" Mom replied. "I haven't taught first grade for years. I really felt like a fish out of water."

MEANING: *Doing something that you aren't used to doing (or that you haven't done before); feeling uncomfortable or as if you don't belong*

ORIGIN: *This popular saying dates back to the 1400s, but its exact origin is unknown. Most believe the expression was used in the* **literal** *sense. In other words, a fish's natural habitat is in the water. A fish out of water is in a very unfamiliar setting!*

Fit as a fiddle

Keneesha was excited. Grandpa was visiting today, and she hadn't seen him for weeks. He'd been in the hospital, and Keneesha had been worried about him.

"Keneesha!" exclaimed Grandpa as he gave her a big hug.

"Hi, Grandpa!" replied Keneesha. "It's great to see you. I was really worried."

"No need to worry about me," said Grandpa, smiling. "I'm fit as a fiddle!"

MEANING: *Healthy or in good shape*
ORIGIN: *This saying was first used in Great Britain in the 1600s. A fiddle is an informal word for violin. The word fit has always meant "in good shape or good health." So a "healthy" violin was in tune and in good shape—it would sound great.*

In your face

It was the beginning of basketball season, and Chris was playing center for the first time. The center on the other team played hard, pushing against Chris and fouling him twice.

"Chris," said the coach afterward, "you did a great job. That player was really in your face, but you didn't let it bother you."

MEANING: *When someone is being aggressive and annoying you*
ORIGIN: *This **slang** phrase became popular in the 1970s in the United States. However, it was likely in use long before that. Most agree that it originally came from players confronting each other during sporting events.*

Lend an ear

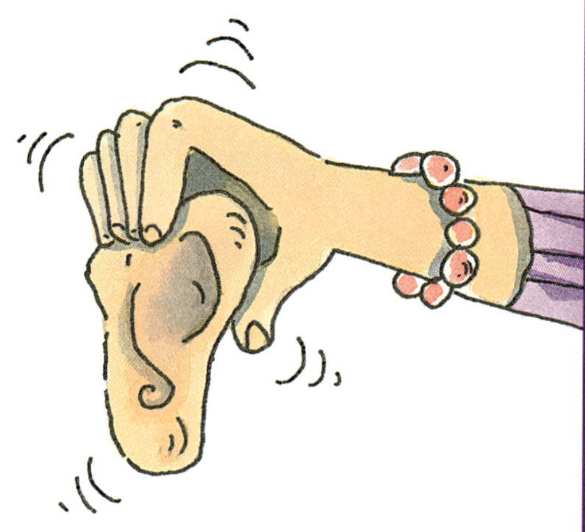

Something was bothering Shania. She wasn't saying much, and she seemed unhappy.

"Is something wrong?" asked Rosa. "You seem awfully quiet."

"No, I'm OK," replied Shania. She looked down and sighed. "I guess it's nothing important."

"Well," said Rosa, "if you want to talk about it, let me know. I'm always ready to lend an ear."

MEANING: *To be a good listener, especially when someone needs to talk about a problem; to pay attention*

ORIGIN: *The phrase was first used around 1600 in Great Britain. The famous playwright William Shakespeare popularized the saying in his works, most notably in the play* Julius Caesar.

Loose cannon

Football season was starting up, and Jen and Zeke were big fans of their school's team.

"Who do you think they're going to start as quarterback?" asked Jen.

"Martinez," said Zeke firmly. "He's so reliable."

"How about Dunn?" said Jen. "He's got an amazing arm."

"Yeah," Zeke replied, "but you never know what he's going to do. He's kind of a loose cannon."

MEANING: *Someone who is unpredictable or acts in unexpected ways; out of control*

ORIGIN: *Sailors on warships have very dangerous jobs. The work was especially dangerous a few hundred years ago with few safety measures in place. Among the greatest threats to sailors was being injured by cannons on their own ship. During storms it was common for cannons to break loose from their ropes and cause serious damage or injuries.*

Mind over matter

Kelly's room was a mess, and Mom said she couldn't go to the movie that night unless it was cleaned up. Kelly looked around at all the clothes and games and toys.

"I'll never get this done in time!" she cried.

"Sure you will," said Mom. "Mind over matter! Tell yourself you can do it, and you'll get it done."

MEANING: *A way to convince yourself that you can do something; the power of the mind is stronger than the body*

ORIGIN: *The Roman poet Virgil is credited with first using this expression in his writings around 19 BC. The phrase became widely used in the 1800s in Great Britain and appeared in scientific publications. Many people believe that the use of* ***alliteration*** *("mind" and "matter" both start with the same letter) also helped make the saying popular.*

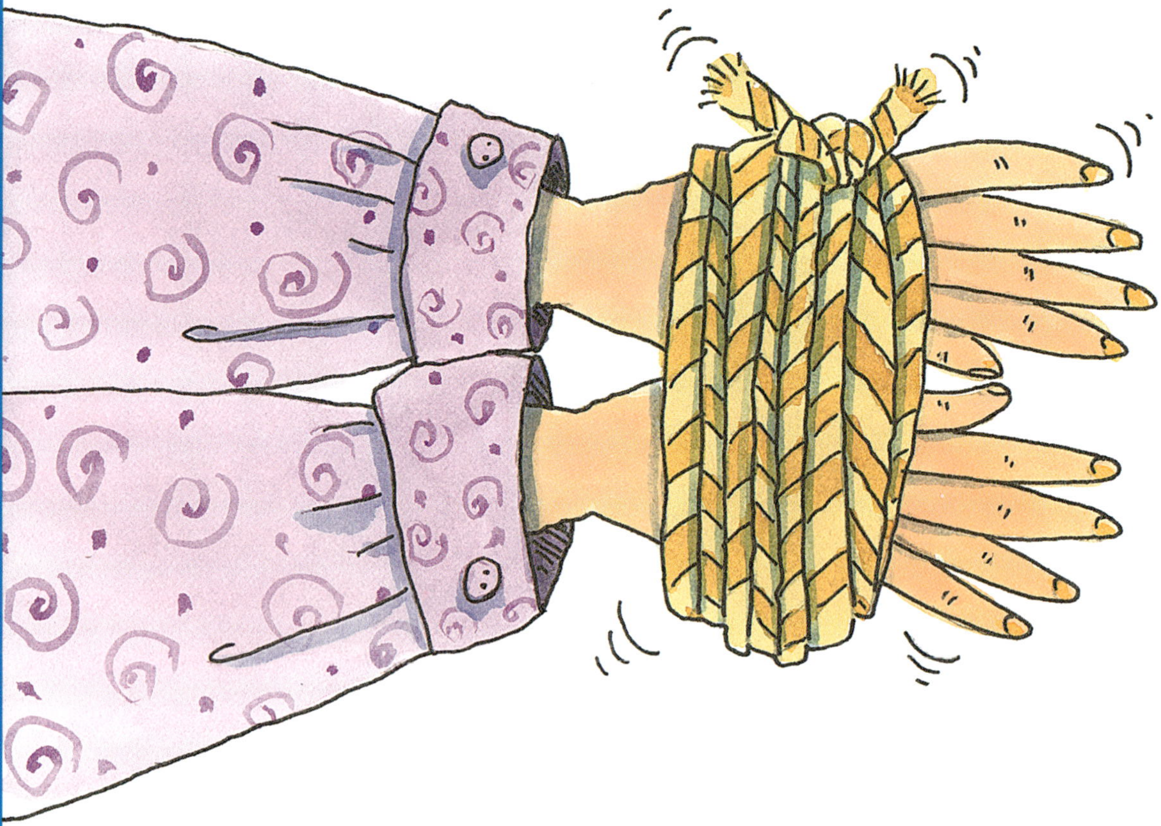

My hands are tied

Annie and Jared were in charge of ordering T-shirts for the drama club, and they were trying to change the design.

"Jared came up with this new idea yesterday," Annie said to Mr. Larsen. "We really like it! Can't we use it instead?"

"Sorry, Annie," said Mr. Larsen, "but we turned in the order on Monday. It's too late to change it. My hands are tied!"

MEANING: *When you can't change something or make a different decision, even if you want to; unable to act*

ORIGIN: *This idiom has been in use since the 1600s, but its exact origin is not known. It is clear, however, that if your hands are bound, or tied together, you are unable to use them. You are prevented from doing something. It is beyond your control.*

Nothing to sneeze at

Luke thought today's baseball game had gone pretty well. He had gotten to pitch for three innings. He'd struck out three batters, and no runs had scored.

"Good job!" said Luke's older brother, Alex.

"Yeah, but I only played three innings," complained Luke.

"Hey," said Alex, "three innings, three strikeouts, no runs—that's nothing to sneeze at!"

MEANING: *Something that shouldn't be ignored; something that is good or important*
ORIGIN: *This expression came about in the United States in the 1800s. Many agree that the phrase first referred to "turning your nose up," meaning that you disapproved of something or were showing* ***scorn****. Eventually the wording changed to "not to be sneezed at" or "nothing to sneeze at" and grew in popularity.*

Over the hill

The house was decorated with balloons and streamers, and the cake was on the table. Everything was ready for Dad's surprise party. It was his fortieth birthday!

"Surprise!" everyone yelled as Dad walked in the door. A big smile stretched across Dad's face. Mom walked over and gave him a hug.

"How does it feel to be over the hill?" she asked with a wink.

MEANING: *To be old; past your prime*

ORIGIN: *Most believe the idiom became popular in the 1950s. The origin likely came from writers at the time comparing a person's lifetime to climbing a hill (or mountain). A young person is climbing up. They reach the top in middle age, and then begin climbing down. They made it up and now they are heading "over the hill."*

Pecking order

Ellis had just started his first job, stocking shelves at the grocery store.

"How did it go?" asked Dad.

"It was confusing," Ellis replied. "Everybody was telling me what to do. The manager, the cashiers—even the other stockers! I didn't know who to listen to."

"Right now you're the new guy," explained Dad. "Pretty soon you'll know where you are in the pecking order."

MEANING: *The order of power in a group of people; knowing who can give orders to whom*

ORIGIN: *This term was first created by biologists in the 1920s. They were studying the relationships and the ruling order, or social status, of flocks of chickens and other birds. It was used to refer to human behavior in the 1950s.*

Pull some strings

Maria was excited! Her favorite singer was going to give a concert in Maria's town. She ran home to ask her parents if she could go.

"I'm sorry, Maria," said Mom. "I heard the tickets are already sold out. But I have a friend who works at the radio station. Maybe she can pull some strings and find us tickets."

MEANING: *To use connections or influence behind the scenes to get something done*
ORIGIN: *The idiom refers to marionettes (string puppets). The movements of these puppets are controlled by someone working behind the scenes. The person pulls the strings connected to different body parts of the puppet, which makes the puppet move.*

Put a sock in it

Robbie's family was on a long road trip, and five-year-old Micah was unhappy.

"This is boring!" he kept saying. "I want to go home."

"Oh, Micah, put a sock in it!" Robbie pleaded. "You're being really annoying."

"You know," said Mom with a laugh. "I remember somebody else who also used to complain on long trips when he was little."

MEANING: *Said to someone to get them to stop talking or complaining*
ORIGIN: *The first printed use of this* **colloquial** *phrase was in a magazine in England in 1919. However, many believe the saying became popular a few years before then during World War I. Soldiers fighting in trenches (ditches and tunnels dug into the ground) would often tell each other to keep quiet or "put a sock in it" so that their enemies didn't hear them.*

Rain or shine

Claire was helping set out food for the family's backyard party. But dark clouds were gathering in the distance.

"What will we do if it rains?" she asked. "Will we have to cancel the party?"

"Oh, no," answered Mom. "There are lots of people coming, and there's a lot of food to eat! This party will go on—rain or shine!"

MEANING: *No matter what happens; no matter what the weather is like*

ORIGIN: *The expression has been in use since the early 1900s. Its origin is unknown, but the longer phrase "come rain or shine" has always referred to weather. It implies that an activity will be carried out, no matter what.*

Stick-in-the-mud

"I don't want to go on a boat ride!" said Ben.

"Ben," sighed his sister, "it's our last day at the lake, and everyone wants to have fun. But you don't want to swim. You don't want to go on a boat ride. You don't want to do anything. Stop being a stick-in-the-mud!"

MEANING: *A person who doesn't want to do fun or new things; someone who is set in their ways*

ORIGIN: *This saying dates back to the early 1700s. The origin is unknown, but many people believe that it likely came from the idea of a wagon's wheels that are stuck in the mud and won't budge.*

Swallow hook, line, and sinker

Caden and Brianna were planning a surprise dinner for their mom's birthday. They needed to get her out of the house while they cooked. Dad offered to help.

"I told her I need help picking out a present for Grandma," he said.

"Did she fall for it?" asked Brianna.

"She swallowed it hook, line, and sinker!" said Dad. "Now, get busy! We'll be back here by six o'clock."

MEANING: *To believe something completely; to be completely taken in by something*
ORIGIN: *This idiom became popular in the 1800s in the United States. Most believe it was based on the older expression "to swallow a gudgeon" used by people in Great Britain. A gudgeon is a small fish that a fisherman uses for bait. A fish that swallows the bait is tricked and captured. Soon the phrase came to mean a person who believes something that isn't true.*

Talk turkey

The first quarter was almost over, and Kyle was having some trouble. His teacher, Mrs. Green, was doing her best to help him.

"All right, Kyle," said Mrs. Green. "Let's talk turkey. You're doing really well in your other subjects, but you're behind in math. What do we need to do to get you caught up?"

MEANING: *To discuss something serious or important; to have an honest, open conversation*
ORIGIN: *The origin is unclear, but this phrase dates back to the early 1800s in the United States. Some people believe that the original meaning referred to early settlers and Native Americans hunting and trading wild turkeys with each other.*

Walking on eggshells

Emily's older sister was nervous about choosing a college, and she was getting cranky with her family.

"Don't let it bother you," Mom said to Emily. "You know your sister's not usually like this. She'll feel better when she makes her decision."

"I know," said Emily, "but it's hard to be around her. I'm afraid of saying the wrong thing. It's like walking on eggshells!"

MEANING: *Being careful not to annoy someone; being very cautious*

ORIGIN: *This expression dates back to the 1500s although the origin is unknown. Some believe it came from the literal sense, meaning that people would walk carefully in a henhouse to avoid stepping on eggshells and disturbing the hens.*

The whole kit and caboodle

The school carnival had lots of fun games, contests, and prizes. Finally it was time for the grand-prize drawing.

"The winner," said Mr. Olson, "is Zach James!"

Zach ran to claim his prize. On the table was a huge basket with toys and treats.

"Which one did I win?" he asked.

"It's all yours!" replied Mr. Olson. "The whole kit and caboodle!"

MEANING: *Everything; the whole thing*

ORIGIN: *The expression has been popular in the United States for well over a hundred years. A kit is a set of things; many believe the "whole kit" refers to the supplies and gear that soldiers carry with them at all times. "Caboodle" likely came from the Dutch word* boodle, *which means a "collection of things" or a "large amount."*

You can't teach an old dog new tricks

Kelsey had been helping Grandma learn how to use her computer. This time, Kelsey was trying to teach her how to open photos she received by email.

"You click here," said Kelsey, "and then there."

"Oh, Kelsey," sighed Grandma. "Sometimes I think I'll never figure this out. You know, you can't teach an old dog new tricks! Thanks for being so patient."

MEANING: *Learning a new approach can be hard, especially if you've been doing something one way for a long time*

ORIGIN: *This proverb can be traced back to a book written in the 1500s. Its origins are based on the literal sense, meaning that people who train animals know that it is easier to train a young animal compared to an older one. Older animals often resist new methods.*

Glossary

alliteration (uh-lit-er-AY-shun): The repetition of the same sound at the beginning of words in a phrase, such as "green grass grows."

colloquial (kuh-LOH-kwee-uhl): Suited for informal, casual conversation or writing.

expression (ek-SPREH-shun): A common saying; telling or showing your thoughts and feelings.

idioms (ID-ee-umz): Phrases or sayings whose meaning can't be understood by their individual words taken separately.

literal (LIT-er-uhl): Concerned with the facts and free from exaggeration; exact.

originated (uh-RIJ-ih-nay-ted): To bring or come into being; to begin.

proverb (PRAH-vurb): A popular, often short saying that expresses something true and wise.

scorn (SKORN): Openly disliking or disrespecting something.

slang (SLANG): Informal speech; giving new meanings to old words or inventing new words.

vulnerable (VUL-ner-ruh-bul): Open to attack or damage; capable of being physically or emotionally wounded.

Wonder More

- Write a short story using an idiom. You can make up a story or use an experience from your own life. For example, if you choose the idiom "every cloud has a silver lining," you could write about discovering something good in an otherwise bad situation.

- In what ways do idioms impact our writing? In your opinion, do they help improve our ability to tell stories and describe events, or are they unnecessary? Explain your reasoning.

- Think of an idiom that isn't in this book and create a new entry. Write your own brief story using the idiom, and draw a picture to go with it. Then write down its meaning and origin. If you don't know the idiom's origin, where could you learn more about it?

- The idiom "mind over matter" from this book is often used to describe overcoming a challenge through your own willpower. What does it mean to you? Partner with someone in your class and come up with examples of when you would use the expression.

Find Out More

In the Library

Fiedler, Heidi, and Kearney, Brendan (illustrator). *The Know-Nonsense Guide to Grammar: An Awesomely Fun Guide to the Way We Use Words!* Laguna Beach, CA: Walter Foster, 2022.

Heinrichs, Ann. *Similes and Metaphors.* Mankato, MN: The Child's World, 2020.

Pearson, Yvonne, and Mernie Gallagher-Cole (illustrator). *Rev Up Your Writing in Fictional Stories.* Mankato, MN: The Child's World, 2016.

Schubert, Susan, and Raquel Bonita (illustrator). *I'll Believe You When . . . Unbelievable Idioms from around the World.* Minneapolis, MN: Lerner, 2020.

On the Web

Visit our website for links about idioms: **childsworld.com/links**

Note to Parents, Caregivers, Teachers, and Librarians: We routinely verify our Web links to make sure they are safe and active sites. So encourage your readers to check them out!

Index